Long Melford School and children, Suffolk 1911

Going to school

"We had a mile to walk to school.
As we walked home to dinner,
we walked four miles each day."

Why do you think children walked to school 80 years ago?

Look carefully at the boys going to school
in this old photograph. They need boots
because the road is not made up like roads today.
It got muddy in winter.

2

"Most days the hobbing iron came into use. Our shoes needed studs or brads."

Most children only had one pair of boots, so they had to be mended at home. The boots were put upside down on a hobbing iron, like the one in the picture. The metal studs were banged in hard. Another name for studs and brads was tacks.

"I wore tacky boots, with tacks in heels and soles. They were very heavy."

Things to do

Start to make a book about school life in 1900. Call the first page *Going to school*. Write about walking to school 80 years ago. Draw a picture. Dress the children in clothes like those in the photographs.

The clothes people wore

"Girls wore black stockings,
laced up boots, dark dresses
and a starched pinafore.
Boys wore knickerbocker suits
with a stiff, white collar."

You can see what the children wore to school
80 years ago by looking at this photograph.
What month was it taken in?

Look for:

— the black stockings
— the dark dresses with long sleeves
— the white pinafores which kept
   their dresses clean
— the knickerbocker trousers, down to the knees,
   worn by the boy on the right
— the boys' stiff collars
— the leather boots, worn by the girl
   on the left
— the wooden clogs, worn by most of the children.
   Most people who lived in the north of England,
   80 years ago, wore wooden clogs.

Whalley, Lancashire 1906

What do you think it felt like to wear clothes like
these, even when it was hot?

4

Whalley
National School
Never
Absent
year ending
July 31st 1906

Things to do

Ask someone older than 70 what they wore when they were your age.
Ask them if they have any photographs to show you.

Draw some pictures of the children outside their school.
Write down what you think about the clothes.

How old is your school?

This school was new about 70 years ago.
There were two gates then, one for the boys
and one for the girls. There was a fence down the middle
of the playground. Children go to this school
today, but the fence has been taken down and they all
go in at one gate. Many of the things children
do in school have changed, too.

The photograph on the right
was taken inside the school.
When was the school opened?

When this school had its
70th birthday, the children
found out about school life
70 years ago.
They talked to some of the
first pupils at the school.

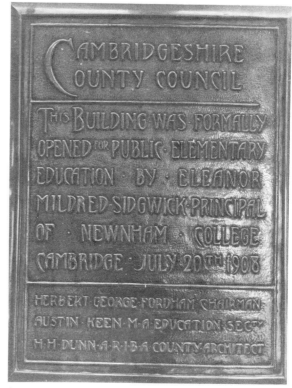

Plaque inside Milton Road School, Cambridge

Milton Road School, Cambridge 1908

Things to do

Look carefully at your school building.
Look inside and outside.
Can you find any clues to tell you
how old your school is?
Write about the age of your school,
in your book.

The classroom

In 1900 school desks were like these.

Barnard Castle Schoolroom, County Durham 1914

"We sat in wooden desks with a shelf underneath.
The seats were fixed to the desk with iron bars.
They had no back rests. We had to bend our knees to get in."

Teachers were strict and made the children sit up
straight with their hands behind their backs.

"Teacher had a cane and used it —
six strokes on the hand or bottom."

Here are some children
in their classroom.
The desks were always
put in straight rows.

Look carefully
at the
two photographs.

Find:

— the blackboards on wooden
   stands called easels
— the gas lights. The gas came
   down the metal pipe.
   The teacher had to pull a
   metal chain and light
   the lamp with a match.
— the bead frame to teach
   the children to count
— the shiny tiles round the wall.

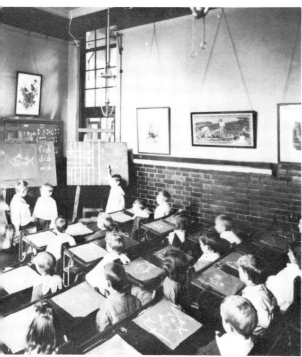

Southfields Infants School, London 1907

Things to do

Look round your classroom. What is different from
the classrooms in the photographs? Make two lists.
Call one list *A classroom now*. Write about your
classroom. Make the other list *A classroom then*.
Write about the classrooms in these photographs.

Keeping warm

"The fireplace was in the long wall, surrounded by an iron fire guard. On wet days, we hung damp clothes to dry on it and at playtime clustered round it to warm our frozen fingers."

Princess Road School, London 1911

A real fire stove like this heated the classroom.
The teacher had to put coal on the fire.
The stove is made of cast iron. The name of the foundry where the stove was made is
CARRON COMPANY 15 UPPER THAMES ST. LONDON EC.

Look for:

— the patterns in the ironwork
— the iron fire guards
— the doors which were opened to let out
   the heat from the fire.

"There were no school dinners. I took bread and cheese and a bottle of cold tea."

The children carried a drink
in this can.
When they took the lid off
they used it as a cup.

Things to do

Does your school have a big chimney?
If it does, it once had a fire like this one.
How is your school heated now?

In your book, draw a picture called *Keeping warm*.
Draw the teacher putting coal on the fire.

Draw and write about the children at
dinner time 80 years ago.

Learning to write

Myddleton School, London 1906

These children are learning to write.
The teacher is pointing to the letter
on the blackboard. Her long stick
is called a pointer. Can you see what
the children are writing on?

"In the infants, we did not write on paper,
but had a little tray filled with sand.
We made our letters and figures
with a stick like a pencil."

The children shook
the sand in the tray
to rub out the writing.

**"Later we had a slate and
a slate pencil which
made a horrible noise
as the whole class worked."**

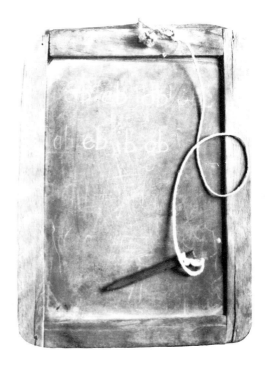

Things to do

Find out about slate.
What else is it used for?

Try to make a sand tray. You could
use the lid of an old shoe box.
Write something in your sand tray.

Pen and ink

**"Later we had pens to dip in ink.
We had to write in copy books. The top line
was printed and we had to make four copies."**

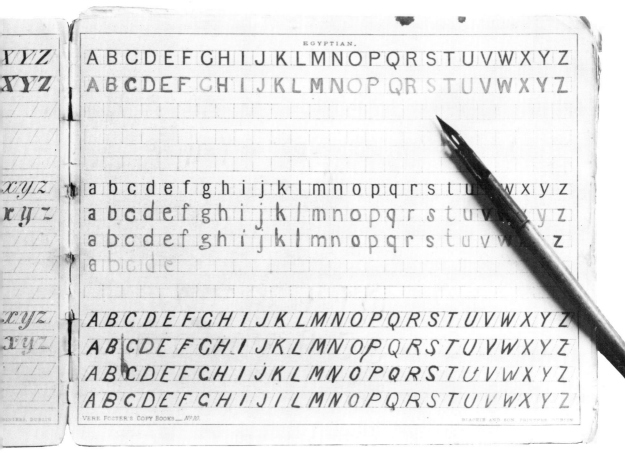

Here is a page from an old copy book.

Are the letters the same as those you write?

There are blots of ink on this page.

This is where the ink dropped off the pen.

Here are the pens
the children used.
The teacher
kept the ink in
a stoneware bottle.
A little ink was put
into the inkwells
in the desks
when they had
a writing lesson.

Things to do

Take some squared paper. Copy the letters from
this copy book. Keep each letter in its own square.

If you have an old pen and some ink
try writing in ink.
Mind you don't make blots or spill the ink!

Put your copy book writing into your book
about school in 1900.

Other lessons

"We had to work hard but we learned a lot. We learned reading, writing, arithmetic, scripture and some history and geography."

These children are learning to read easy words. They point to a word in their books and all read it out loud at the same time.
Look at the classroom wall. The words they are learning to read are put up on the classroom wall.

"We had fifty spellings to learn every week. Here are some of the words I remember having to learn:

you	yew	ewe
bow	bough	
doe	dough."	

Upper Lloyd Street School, Manchester 1913

"We chanted our tables every day, from two to five times. We counted in twos and fives most days."

Some of the lessons they learnt by heart, like this history verse:
"1666,
London burned like rotten sticks."

"We learned little pieces of poetry and some songs, too."

"Gentle Jesus, meek and mild,
  Look upon a little child;
  Pity my simplicity,
  Suffer me to come to thee."

Things to do

Ask someone over 70 what they did in scripture and arithmetic.
Ask them what songs and poems they learnt at school.
Can they write them down for you? Copy them into your book.
Read them to your friends.

Drill

Here are two photographs of Drill lessons 80 years ago.

Hague Street School, Miles Platting, Manchester 1911

Did the children change their clothes and shoes for Drill?
What are the white lines on the floor for?

**"We all did our arm stretching at the same time.
Sometimes we drilled in our desks,
or in the space between our desks."**

In good weather the children did Drill in the playground.

Things to do

Try out some Drill with your friends.
Make them stand in a straight line.
Call out "1...2...3...4". Make sure all the
children do the same thing at the same time.

In your book, write about Drill 80 years ago.
How are your P.E. lessons different from Drill?

Look for
the teacher
shouting out
instructions.
What has he told
them to do?

Gopsall Street School,
London 1906

Special days

Every May, there were two special days at school. Visitors came to watch the children.

"On May Day, we had a grand tea in the school after the crowning of the May Queen, and danced round the Maypole."

Southfields Infants School, London 1906

Look for the May Queen in this photograph.
She has a long white dress and a crown of flowers.

Here are the words to a May Day song:

"Come lasses and lads, get leave of your dads,
And away to the Maypole hie,
For every he has got him a she,
And the fiddler's standing by.
For Willie shall dance with Jane,
And Johnny has got his Joan,
To trip it, trip it, trip it, trip it, trip it up and down."

May 24th was
Empire Day.

**"On Empire Day
we used to sing
patriotic songs in
the playground
watched by our
mothers, and salute
the Union Jack."**

These children are
dressed up for
Empire Day.

Look for:

— the flag
— the girl dressed
   as Britannia
— children dressed
   in clothes from
   India, Scotland
   and Wales.

Romsey School, Cambridge 1917

Things to do

What is a patriotic song?
Do you ever sing them at school today?

Write down the words of a patriotic song.

Prizes

''You had to be
'Never absent,
never late'.''

This certificate was given to
Ronald Mitchell in August 1905.
How did he earn it?

This girl won two medals because
she went to school every day
for two years.

Here are some more school medals.

— left, how did Florence Clark earn her medal?
— what does "good conduct" mean?
Who was the King of England in 1911?

Things to do

Ask an old person you know if they ever won a prize at school.
What was the prize? Why did they win it?

Write down what children win certificates for at school today.

Draw and colour a certificate for school 80 years ago.
Draw another one for your school today.

School 80 years ago

Flint Street School, London 1908

Many old people will tell you that your schooldays
are the happiest days of your life.

Do you think you would have liked going to school 80 years ago?

The following museums have old schoolrooms as part of their display:

North of England Open Air Museum,
   Beamish Hall, Stanley, County Durham
Staffordshire County Museum, Shugborough,
   near Stafford
Museum of East Anglian Life, Stowmarket, Suffolk

British Schools Museum, Hitchin,
   Hertfordshire (visits by appointment
   to Jill E. Grey, Hitchin 59956)
Museum of Childhood, High Street,
   Edinburgh.